Andi,

I'm sorry to hear of Dylan's suffering. I hope you may find comfort in this book. You are loved.

Robin

As Someone Dies

As Someone Dies
A Handbook for the Living

Elizabeth A. Johnson

Hay House, Inc.
Carson, CA

Published and distributed in the United States by:
Hay House, Inc., 1154 E. Dominguez St., P.O. Box 6204, Carson, CA 90749-6204
(800) 654-5126

Edited by: Jill Kramer   Designed by: Highpoint, Claremont, CA

Library of Congress Cataloging-in-Publication Data

Johnson, Elizabeth
　　　　　As someone dies : a handbook for the living / Elizabeth A.
　　Johnson. -- (New and rev. ed.)
　　　　　　　　p.　cm.
　　　　　Includes bibliographical references.
　　　　　ISBN 1-56170-221-8
　　　　　1. Death.　2. Bereavement.　I. Title.
　　HQ1073.J64　1995
　　155.9'37--dc20　　　　　　　　　　　　　　　　　　　　95-8729
　　　　　　　　　　　　　　　　　　　　　　　　　　　　CIP

ISBN 1-56170-221-8

99 98 97 96 95　5 4 3 2 1
First Printing by 21st Century Emporium
First Hay House Printing, 1987
First Printing, Revised Edition, November 1995

Printed in the United States of America

With special appreciation to Kim Myers.

This book is for my Mother.

Death puts Life into perspective.

— Ralph Waldo Emerson

Stripped of all purple robes,
Stripped of all golden lies,
I will not be afraid.
Truth will persevere through death.

— John Masefield

Remember, death is not a failure. Everyone dies;
it's part of the process of life.

— Louise L. Hay

CONTENTS

Foreword by Louise L. Hay .... *xi*

Preface .... *xiii*

Chapter 1   Life 1

Chapter 2   Before 7

Chapter 3   During............................ 25

Chapter 4   After 35

Chapter 5   The Death of a Child................ 47

Chapter 6   Death in a Child's Life.............. 61

Chapter 7   The Death of a Pet................. 67

Chapter 8   Sudden Death..................... 71

APPENDIX

Recommended Reading........................... 81

Self-Help Resources.............................. 86

About the Author................................ 96

This is my death...and it will profit me to understand it.

— Anne Sexton

FOREWORD

Shortly after I published my book, *I Love My Body*, in 1985, I knew that it was time to expand the Hay House library and bring in the works of other authors who support my philosophy of life. Two weeks after that decision, God brought Elizabeth Johnson to me.

At this time, with the increase of cancer and aids, many more people are leaving the planet. Some of them are quite young, and there is a greater need for understanding the process of death. No longer can we hide our heads and pretend death does not exist.

Elizabeth truly understands that death is another experience of life. She is there for us in those times of need, bringing us practical suggestions. I have used some of them myself when visiting those who are seriously ill. There may come a time when we need to be able to say to a loved one: "It's all right to go; you can leave now." Elizabeth helps us to say this without guilt. There is much wisdom in this book, and it has served as a beautiful source of inspiration for readers since its initial publication.

I am very pleased to present the new and revised edition of Elizabeth Johnson's book. The beauty and gentleness expressed in *As Someone Dies* will be a comfort to many.

— Louise L. Hay
   September 1995

To every thing there is a season, and a time for
every purpose under the heaven: a time to be
born and a time to die.

— Ecclesiastes 3:1

And when he shall die
take him
and cut him out in little stars
and he will make the face of heaven
so fine
that all the world
will be in love with the night
and pay no worship
to the garish sun.

— William Shakespeare
Romeo and Juliet

When I am dead, my dearest,
Sing no sad songs for me.

— Christina Rossetti

PREFACE

Death is not unusual. Every single person in the entire world will, one day, leave the earth, make the transition, expire, pass over, pass on, graduate, die. It is as normal and natural as birth—both a universal act and a very personal experience.

While the loved one (anyone with whom we are spending this precious time) is busily involved in the dying process, the rest of us are saddened, angered, confused, nervous, and sometimes even embarrassed witnessing the intimacy of the procedure. We will ourselves to be there, yet stand by feeling helpless. What can I do/say to help... and what if I do/say the wrong thing?

It's a double-edged sword—we are so immersed in our own fears that we emotionally pull back from the dying, and we are so concerned with the dying that we neglect our own nurturing.

Many fine books have been written on the subject of death and dying; some are listed in the Appendix in the Recommended Reading section. The subject of "death education" is advancing rapidly, with a broad spectrum of scientists, psychologists, teachers, counselors, philosophers, doctors, and nurses who are researching and questioning the death, near-death, and after-death experiences. They endeavor to learn ever more about the death experience and to pass on that knowledge to others in order to eliminate that most basic of human fears—the fear of not being on the planet any longer.

Yet, when the immediate experience centers on *your* loved one, theories are hard to remember, and books seem to hold little meaning.

This handbook is designed to help you: 1) during the stressful days of a loved one's impending death; 2) after the death to allow grief to heal the sense of loss; and 3) to build a better understanding of death as it pertains to life.

Through the entire process, whether it is called *death* or *transition,* it is important to remember that each of us is composed of four elements: body, mind, emotions, and Life Force. The one who is passing away is not just his body; just as you, during this very emotional time, are not just your feelings.

This handbook has been written to assist all of us. It has been especially influenced by the lives and deaths of my father, my brother, and Mr. Max Whiteshoes, my cat.

— Elizabeth A. Johnson
    September 1995

Death is the last enemy: once we've gotten past that
I think everything will be all right.

— Alice Thomas Ellis

God is not a God of the dead, but of the living, for in
his sight, all are alive. The Spirit is both birthless and
deathless. The Principle of Life cannot know death.
The experience of dying is but the laying off of an old
garment, and the donning of a new one. There are
bodies celestial and bodies terrestrial, there is a
material body and a spiritual body. This spiritual
body is the resurrection body.

— Ernest Holmes
The Science of Mind

Everyone desires to live longer,
but no one wants to be old.

— Jonathan Swift

CHAPTER
ONE

Life

*We see the world piece by piece, as the sun, the
moon, the animal, the tree: but the Whole, of which
these are the shining parts, is the Soul.**

Brain and Mind, Body and Soul

As members of the human race, we primarily perceive
life through our senses. We get our information about
people, places, things, and events from what we witness
and experience as we move through the days of our lives.

We are receptors, or receivers, of data about what is
going on around us and around the world. This information, to a great degree, helps to form what we think of as
our *self*—that is, our "beingness," which includes personality, thoughts, emotions, actions, reactions, and our general
outlook on life. In other words, the information we receive
from our senses helps to form who we think we "are."

Since you are reading this book, you *are*. You exist.
You know that you exist because you see the words, feel
the paper, hear sounds around you, perhaps even smell
dinner cooking. At the same time, your brain is quickly
translating letters into words, into sentences, into meaning,
and you are also mentally registering other environmental
stimuli and perhaps experiencing feelings of the past and
present, or even projecting into the future. The fact that

this entire process is happening automatically and simultaneously is quite remarkable.

You are even more remarkable.

> *We live in succession, in division, in parts,*
> *in particles. Meanwhile, within man is the soul of the*
> *Whole, the wise silence, the universal beauty,*
> *to which every part and particle is equally*
> *related: the eternal ONE.**

We are all, equally, a part of the Eternal One. We are, in fact, not only a part of the Eternal One, but also, the Eternal One lives and expresses through us, as us. While you are busy with your particular life on earth, the Eternal One (or Infinite Mind, or God) is, all the while, expressing Itself as you.

What does this mean? It means that you and I are so much more than we think or feel we are. We are each more than our thoughts, more than our feelings, more than our actions. We are each connected to the Infinite Mind, or God, or Eternal One. The soul of each of us is the Soul of the Infinite Mind.

Now, the word *soul* (*l'ame, psyche, el alma, ziel, kokoru, die Seele, sjel, l'anima*) is simply a term that now seems to relate as much to food, music, and religion as it does to the Eternal, Infinite Mind. Yet the soul does express in each individual through, or as, the mind. You could say that the mind is the soul, inspiring the person.

But where is a person's soul? It cannot be found in the physical body, like tonsils, because it is not *of* the body, yet it operates the body.

Likewise, where is a person's mind? The mind cannot be found in the brain, yet the brain is a tool of the mind.

A man is a facade of a temple
*wherein all wisdom and good abide.**

There is One Eternity, therefore, one Universal Mind, which is Eternal. Our individualized mind, as an expression of Universal Mind, is eternal. Our body is the temple of the mind/soul and, as matter, is not eternal.

Our individual "being" is a result of Infinite Mind (that is, God) incarnating into the form of each and every one of us. This is creation. Just as Infinite Mind creates by thought, so do we. Since you, the person, are alive (and reading this material), you are also constantly creating through your thoughts. Thought creates. Life is a rich passage of ideas, feelings, sights, sounds, experiences, and all forms of communication. While *receiving* information and influences, you are also *creating* experiences (both challenging and rewarding) because Infinite Mind, of which your mind is an aspect, continually creates by thought. So do you.

When the activity of the brain ceases, mind moves on to further create. It does not simply die or go away. It cannot. Mind/soul, as part of the Infinite Intelligence of the Universe, is Eternal. You—the individualization of the Infinite—are Eternal. No soul can be damned or lost, just as no mind can die. The Infinite is far beyond even acknowledging that concept. The Infinite continues to create—and incarnate—Universally.

The soul looketh steadily forwards,
creating a world before her,
leaving worlds behind her....
The soul knows only the soul: the web of
*events is the flowing robe in which she is clothed.**

There is comfort here, and safety, and great love. The mind/soul leaves the body to move *forward*. The essence of each person moves into larger growth, into more multicolored experiences, to incarnate again. The uniqueness of each of us continues in ways and spheres we do not now remember. Yet the essence continues to grow Eternally.

Now, I wish you to feel and know and be all the qualities of the Infinite that are found in you, in me, in everyone. This is the true essence of you. It never dies, and it is you forever more. Remarkable you:

Love   Light   Life   Peace
Power   Beauty   Joy

(*The italicized excerpts in this chapter are from Ralph Waldo Emerson's essay, "The Over-Soul.")

I put aside my concept of reality.
I am willing to trust that that which
now seems beyond my grasp is the
unseen but certain Love, which leads
my beloved to his or her perfect place.

Applaud my friends, the comedy is over.

— Ludwig van Beethoven
(on his deathbed)

And now the time has come when we must depart;
I to my death, you to go on living.
But which of us is going to the better fate
is unknown to all except God.

— Socrates

We are all resigned to death;
it's life we aren't resigned to.

— Graham Greene

CHAPTER
TWO

Before

Why?

Although it is impossible to fully answer the question, "Why?," it seems also impossible not to ask it. We want to know why death is happening to someone we love. We want to know why death is happening to *us*.

We may angrily shake our fists at the heavens, cry bitter tears at the impending loss, anesthetize ourselves with alcohol, drugs, whatever. The question remains: Why is the person I love dying? Why? Why? Why?

Write down the question. Keep a private, personal journal or diary. When you ask yourself why, write both the question and what you feel to be the answer(s). Along with "I don't know," you will come up with many answers—and these answers can reveal to you closeted thoughts and feelings which, when written and examined (that is, realized), lose all their power and control over you.

These "answers" may include feelings of loss, betrayal, abandonment, punishment, fear, and so on. Be sure to know that any feelings you have during this time are all right. There is nothing "wrong" with emotions, and there is nothing "wrong" with you. You are not a bad person because you may feel fearful, angry, or vulnerable.

By using the question, "Why?" as a focus, and by writing down your thoughts and feelings, you are doing a great service to yourself and the dying person in your life.

You are bringing to the hospital or sick bed a sense of clarity about yourself. And, although your feelings will alter and change as time goes on, you are showing love for all concerned by allowing yourself private moments to express how you honestly feel. By doing so, you are permitting yourself to release your thoughts outwardly, yet not verbally.

You need not share your personal writings with anyone, although you may if you wish. Be with yourself for a few moments each day, and really let your thoughts and feelings out!

Hour by Hour

If one could imagine an "ideal" transition situation, it would probably involve a very old person, gently slipping away at home, surrounded and supported by loving family and friends. More often, however, we are presented with a hospital or hospice environment where we sit with a loved one for hours at a time while they doze, fidget, experience pain, or simply reflect in silence.

What does this time mean to you? And to them? It can provide some of the most memorable, meaningful hours in both your lives. It is not necessary to feel you must "do" anything—your physical presence reveals your love.

Yet, if we wish to feel useful, there are some things all of us can do to help out at this time.

First, take your cue from the one who is dying. Allow this person to decide if he wants to talk or not. Expressions of thoughts and feelings ought to be up to him. Pay attention to what he has to say. If the language is unintelligible, listen with interest anyway, because some communication is taking place. If this person does not care to converse with you, then do something for yourself—read the newspaper or a book, do needlepoint or crossword puzzles.

Next, allow your friend or loved one to feel very safe with you. Offer to hold his hand, stroke his arm, massage his hands and feet, comb his hair. The physical sensation of touching brings with it comfort and a sense of security. But make sure you ask his permission before you attempt to do any of these things. The person may simply not be in the mood.

If there are moments when you just don't know what to say, then just smile, and *think* the words you would *like* to say.

During this time, it is very important for you to be aware of your own needs. Although your focus will no doubt remain on the other person, it's fine to take a walk around the block or go to the cafeteria for a while. Physical movement and changes in your environment will energize you and help to lessen your stress, as well as the feeling of being drained.

Whether you are in the company of this person or not, take some time occasionally to run through your senses mentally. While the person naps, or perhaps as you go to or from the hospital, be aware of each separate sense, and mentally record what it is doing:

— What do you see? What color is the sky? What different shapes are the trees?

— Identify the sounds that you hear. How many different sounds are there in your immediate environment?

— What smells are present? Are they pleasant or not?

— Do you have a taste in your mouth? What is it?

— How does the breeze/sun/air feel on your skin?

— What are your hands touching, and how does it feel to you?

This sense evaluation sharpens your awareness of the things around you and increases your own mental alertness.

The easiest thing for you to do for yourself during these hours is to be aware of your breathing. Slightly exaggerate your inhaling and exhaling on a regular basis. This practice increases oxygen in your system and aids in calming stressed nerves.

Although you may feel you can take care of yourself "later," doing these things for yourself now increases your immediate ability to endure, and helps to provide a natural defense against depression. Know that the hours *will* pass.

Between grief and nothing I will take grief.

— William Faulkner

Pre-Grief

I remember a family dinner when I was a very young child. For no apparent reason, I suddenly began weeping hot, heavy tears in deep sobs. My wonderful Irish grandmother took me on her lap and simply said, "'Tis nothing. 'Tis but an angel passing over."

Many years later, I was struck by an overwhelmingly profound sadness one day. My dad had cancer, yet he was doing quite well. I knew in my heart that he would eventually die and, although the actualization of his passing would not be for months to come, the grief I was experiencing overcame me beyond any rational level. It would not be lessened or shaken away by any of my attempts at keeping a happy face and a sunny attitude.

Pre-grief, or the anticipatory feeling of loss, can happen at any time in one's life, and the factors that trigger this emotional upheaval are not always clear.

Many of us have felt teary-eyed when gazing at a beautiful sunset, a cherubic little baby, or something equally miraculous in our world. Yet pre-grief is very different. It is deeper, sadder, and longer lasting.

Of course there may be moments of grieving before a loved one's actual transition. This is natural when our thoughts jump ahead of time, and we begin to imagine how we are going to feel after that person is gone. To assist in moving beyond these moments, firmly and quickly stop anticipating. Do something else. Write out a shopping list; pick up something to read. Turn on some loud rock music; jump in the shower. Use your workout equipment; go for a walk.

I am not suggesting that you deny the emotion, but rather, simply do not allow it to consume you. There is time now for you to be with your loved one, to talk together or simply sit in each other's presence. You need not spend this precious time being stuck or immobilized by pre-grief. For the good of all concerned, it is wise to try to live this time in your life in the most productive way that you can. Remember that you cannot keep two opposing thoughts in your mind at the same time, so hold on to all the positive thoughts of the present; therefore, any negative thoughts of the future will not be able to get in.

Talking to others can help a great deal. Shared grief brings shared love and understanding.

At times, sudden, unexplained sadness may strike for no apparent reason at all. At that moment, catch up with your thoughts. Where are they taking you? Are you perhaps imagining your own death? Feel free now to repeat: "'Tis but an angel passing over," and imagine in detail the beauty of that perfect angel.

When I think of death, and of late the idea
has come with alarming frequency, I seem at peace
with the idea that a day will dawn when I will no
longer be among those living in this valley of strange
humors. I can accept the idea of my own demise,
but I am unable to accept the death of anyone else.
I find it impossible to let a friend or relative go into
that country of no return. Disbelief becomes my close
companion, and anger follows in its wake.

    I answer the heroic question "Death, where
is thy sting?" with "It is here in my heart and mind
and memories...."

    Also, when I sense myself filling with rage at
the absence of a beloved, I try as soon as possible to
remember that my concerns and questions, my efforts
and answers should be focused on what I did or can
learn from my departed love. What legacy was left
which can help me in the art of living a good life?

— from *Won't Take Nothing for My Journey Now,*
by Maya Angelou

I know what will happen when I die.
Everyone will come over and tell my husband
what a nice lady I was.
Then they'll go home.

— A.J.

Whenever I think about my own death I have this
great urge to go out and buy the theme from the
movie, Rocky, *then call the undertaker to make*
sure it's played at my funeral.

— J.P.

Life does not cease to be funny when people die any
more than it ceases to be serious when people laugh.

— George Bernard Shaw

The Other Person

Each death is as individual and unique as each life. Although we know that the Life Force (or Spirit, Soul, God, Source, Force, Energy, Infinite Mind—that is, the Thing that enlivens all things) withdraws from the body, we do not know exactly how. There is a different design, a different process, for each individual.

When the terminally ill, distinguished, intelligent gentleman becomes cantankerous and abusive, it is simply part of his own individual process of letting go of this world. Likewise, when the gentle, devoted wife and mother glares in angry, defiant aggression, it is one of the steps she must take to complete her life.

We do not really know why this happens, but you may witness moments of total personality reversal in your loved one. Remember that this phenomenon is part of the person's unique dying process and, although it may be directed at you, it really has nothing to do with you on a personal level. It could be a reaction to medication; it could be a reaction to internal anger and fear; or it is perhaps simply a step the loved one takes in his specific way of dying.

If the person is cranky, angry, or abusive, be both honest and fair. Gently say, "I love you. And please don't speak to me that way." In this manner, you are helping the person move through and get out of that stage of the process.

There may be times when the person seems to be "talking crazy," hallucinating, or going senile. He may speak of people, places, and events as though everything was happening now. Or, in sleep, his hands may move busily, appearing to be directing traffic, hammering nails, counting money, and so on.

The wonderful makeup of body, mind, emotions, and Life Force now enables the person to think, feel, and imagine on many different levels, in many different areas. Remember that what he is saying and doing is very real to him. Due to a freer expression of the subconscious, your loved one may be speaking and acting out in symbols, which, though foreign to you, hold considerable meaning to him.

Rather than trying to coerce the person back to the "reality" of the hospital room or ignoring his rambling (which, in effect, means that you're ignoring him), try to play along.

In my own experience (see Chapter 3), my brother woke from a nap one afternoon and said:

"Honey, you've got to move your car."

"Why?" I asked.

"Because it's blocking the fire wall."

"Can't I move it later?"

"No, can't you see?" He waved his arm in the direction of the television set. "It's blocking the fire wall!"

"Ok, I'll move it now."

So I got up, walked out of the room, walked back into the room, and said, "I moved the car."

"Thanks." He smiled broadly. "I really appreciate it."

It did him good to participate in a scene that made no sense to me but was vivid and real to him.

Also, be aware that your loved one, even when apparently asleep, can hear what is going on in the room. He is also very involved in the biggest adventure of life, equaled only by birth. So discourage a visiting Aunt Rosie from rattling on about her bridge club, and say only what you would want your loved one to hear.

Quiet Moments

The finest communication we have is in our thoughts, and we can give ourselves the freedom not to speak at times.

Look at your loved one's hand. Hold it. Look at the skin, veins, nails. Appreciate it as being *a part* of the person you know.

Look at your loved one's face. Look at the structure, the color, the lines. Appreciate it as being *a part* of the person you know.

Scan down the length of the bed, and look at the outline of your loved one's body. Appreciate it as being *a part* of the person you know.

Now, gently inhale and exhale four or five times. Look at your loved one and *know*—tell yourself with conviction—that what you are seeing is *a part* of the person you love.

Look beyond the body. Know that your loved one is eternal. Appreciate that. Know that *you* are eternal. Appreciate that. Breathe deeply.

Feeling Helpless

Watching someone die and not being able to do anything to prevent the process from occurring takes an emotional toll on us. We may feel ourselves to be the victims of our own helplessness. Yet, by participating in the transformation process, by being there *with* the person and *for* the person, we are hardly helpless. We are helpers.

We may fluff pillows, hold hands, talk, listen, help with sips of water. And we can even do more:

1. Either in the loved one's room or elsewhere, sit quietly and close your eyes. Be aware of your breathing. In your mind, select a color that represents comfort and safety to you. Whatever color you choose is fine. Now, imagine that you can surround your loved one in this color. Imagine that you can see the person comfortably surrounded and protected by the color you have chosen. Hold this image in your mind, and be aware that you

are breathing. When it is comfortable for you, open your eyes.

2. Select a piece of soothing classical or soft music that appeals to you. With the music playing, sit quietly and close your eyes. Be aware of your breathing. Now, imagine that you can direct each note of the music completely through the body of your loved one. Picture the person in your mind, and imagine that each note of music travels through him, bringing tranquility, safety, and comfort to every part of his being. Continue to visualize this process until the music ends. Be aware of your breathing and, when it is comfortable for you, open your eyes.

3. Whenever the whirlwind of thoughts and feelings seems to overwhelm you, sit quietly and close your eyes. Feel your feet supported firmly by the floor. Breathe deeply. Imagine that each breath you take calms and soothes you. The first breath you take goes to the very soles of your feet, the second breath fills your feet, the third goes directly to your ankles, the fourth settles in your lower calves, the fifth goes to your upper calves, the sixth to your knees....and so on, until you are totally filled to the top of your head with new air. Continue breathing and, when it feels comfortable to you, open your eyes.

4. Take special care to drink eight to ten glasses of water per day during this period, particularly in a hospital environment where the air tends to be

dry. Water stimulates and energizes the body by helping to rid it of toxic waste.

5. It is good to cry. It is very good to cry.

6. It is okay to feel that you hate Life/God/the Universe. Life/God/The Universe does not take this as a personal affront. It knows that this feeling will—in time—pass for you.

Near-Death Experiences

The summer I was seven years old, I was playing in the lake with my friends one day. I guess I must have walked out too far or something, because suddenly there was nothing beneath my feet. I clearly remember bobbing up and down underwater. And then I was surrounded by the most beautiful little light beams, hundreds of them. I just knew that they were angels, and I felt very good. I even thought it was funny that angels were underwater instead of in heaven, so I started to laugh.

Obviously, someone pulled me out of the lake, and I still swim today. Yet the feeling and image of those wonderful angel-lights has remained with me. It's a very comforting, supportive memory.

Fortunately, much is being written and discussed now about near-death experiences (NDEs), and our consciousness seems to be elevating far above the old concept of the aloneness of death and the darkness/nothingness of "the other side."

In the majority of cases of people who "came back" to life as we know it on Earth, there is mention of the light or some type of brightness, as well as feelings of both calmness and alertness. There is, indeed, something wondrous awaiting us when we venture forward from our present place—something in which fear has no part.

My mother underwent surgery a few years after my father died. She later told me that during the operation, she had seen and spoken to Dad in a very well-lit area. He told her that she had to go back because there was much more for her to do. In the 20 years since that experience, my mom's life has been spent both taking care of others who needed her and traveling throughout the United States and Europe. So there was, and continues to be, a lot more for her to do here.

It is helpful and soothing to recall stories of near-death experiences when you are working through the transition or impending transition of a loved one. The understanding that there is brightness rather than darkness, and great love as opposed to judgment, awaiting each and every one of us, can make it easier for you to say goodbye.

I was in the emergency room very high up near the ceiling. Looking down I could see myself lying on the bed, and John, my husband, standing beside me. I noticed that the bald spot on the top of his head was getting bigger. Then there was a lot of bright light, and a rather large voice said to me, "Oh no, not yet. The world needs more of YOU!" I was immediately pushed into the me on the bed. My eyes flew open, and I looked at John's face. He was crying.

— Jo Anne

Hospices

Do largely to the excellent efforts of Dr. Elisabeth Kübler-Ross, the hospice movement has grown tremendously in the United States. Initially developed in England, hospices provide care and comfort for terminally ill people. Family and friends are encouraged to visit often and stay long. Trained staff members meet the needs of the dying with concern and respect.

Many hospitals are now converting wings into hospice areas. Whenever possible, room is made for a family member or friend to stay the night so that the person approaching death need not spend dark hours alone.

You are strongly encouraged to explore the hospice alternatives in your area and examine that possibility for your loved one. We are growing beyond the days when it was very common and natural for the dying to be at home with the support of those dearest to them. Yet we can still extend our caring for family and friends to include the comfort and safety of a hospice environment.

No one dies alone.

— Elisabeth Kübler-Ross

Mark and I talked a lot near the end about what we thought the other side of the clouds looked like. I was right there with him the morning he found out.

— Ed

*When you love someone, it means you want them to
go where they will be happiest, even if that
means leaving you.*

— Anonymous

Right to Die/Assisted Deaths

Does a person facing imminent death have the right to leave earth when and how he wishes, rather than wait out the time? Does someone else have the right or responsibility to assist in this transition?

There is controversy. There is confusion. There are laws. The media is making much of these issues, and lines are being drawn. I do not now know what the answers are. However, we can know with certainty that the eternal vastness of Universal Mind holds no controversy, no confusion, and that Infinite Law supersedes any laws made by humans. There is no Lord of terror or punishment or judgment. God is love. God loves each and every one of us more than we can imagine. The aspect of God that is us, our soul, does not diminish as a result of human behavior. That soul grows and develops here while awaiting reunion with its Source.

Of course it is our privilege to have personal opinions and preferences. Yet, it is wise to remember that each death, each time a soul goes home, is a uniquely personal, private matter between the soul and its Creator. The physical body, the person we knew, is no longer the issue, for their true life is on a much higher level now.

If it is possible, before you are faced with a right-to-die dilemma, investigate a Living Will with your loved ones. Make decisions together. Even though it may feel awkward to all of you, be clear in your understanding of individual desires.

Be assured that the Infinite Universe knows the pure truth in everything that is happening. It does not judge. You don't have to either.

> *God loves my dear friend.*
> *The moment of their joyous*
> *reunion is lovingly made*
> *between them.*
> *Thank you for loving my friend.*

Keeping Death a Secret

Because of its tender love and great understanding of the earth, the element of the person called "body" often doesn't want to leave. Sometimes...it takes time.

Yet, there is a higher aspect of the loved one, the Life Force, that wills this person to move on, to make this transformation complete.

So, even if it has never been discussed, death is not a dark, painful secret—and the dying know that best.

> *Waiting are they? Waiting are they? Well,*
> *goddam 'em, let 'em wait!*

> — Ethan Allen, to his physician,
> who said, "General, I fear the
> angels are waiting for you."

In my Father's house
are many mansions.
I now let go and allow my
friend to step into another room.

I looked at the city of the living and said to myself, "That place belongs to the few." Then I looked upon the city of the dead and said, "That place, too, belongs to the few. Oh Lord, where is the haven of all people?"

As I said this, I looked toward the clouds, mingled with the sun's longest and most beautiful golden rays. I heard a voice within me saying, "Over there!"

— from *The City of the Dead,* by Kahlil Gibran

To die will be an awfully big adventure.

— J.M. Barrie

CHAPTER
THREE

During

The Light

I had seen my older brother a year before on an infrequent visit home to upstate New York. He was going on 40, and we joked about it. He was the type of guy who grows into 40 handsomely—physically strong and humanly kind, with some small lines around the eyes and dark hair graying slightly and evenly. He took my mom and me to Thanksgiving dinner in his new truck, a Chevy, I think—one of the sleek ones. Suede jacket, nice boots, neatly pressed jeans. I described him to friends in Los Angeles as the "upstate New York cowboy."

Now it was November 8th, almost a year since I realized he was handsome. He had been diagnosed only six weeks before—with cancer. It wouldn't heal. He didn't look the same.

I was alone with him early that morning, and we held hands.

"Honey," he said, "you've got to help me."

"Tom, I am helping you. We're all helping you."

"But," he said, with a tense body and desperate eyes, "you've *got* to help me."

And I knew that it was happening. I thought of all the moments in the past few days I had wished it had happened when I wasn't there. Now it was happening—and I was very much there.

"Tom, I am helping you. We're all helping you. Can you feel us loving you and helping you?"

"No. God, help me..."

"God is helping you, Tom. God is right here with you, helping you. You're safe. You're very safe. We're all here helping you. You *can* feel us helping you, can't you?"

He looked at me slowly and carefully. "Yes...everyone...*is* helping me...."

"Yes, we're all helping you. You're safe. You're very safe."

He looked away, then back at me with the start of a smile.

"I'm safe...I *am* safe...you're all doing a good job...."

He was calmer now, still clutching my hand. We looked at each other for a long time.

"You're safe. You are very, very safe." I kept repeating it.

"I'm safe...yes, I'm safe." Tom started to relax.

Then he put out his other hand and pulled me to his chest and hugged me with more strength than his weakened skeletal form could possibly possess—the body bidding a strong farewell to the earth, and him saying goodbye to me.

Our mother had been spending nights in his hospital room so he would not be alone. Although she had just left the hospital when I arrived, I phoned her to come back.

Now I let *him* hold my hand, in case he wanted the freedom to let go.

"Tom, can you see the light?"

He seemed to look beyond me. Then, almost casually, he said, "Yeah...there it is. I can see the light."

"Tom...can you go to the light?"

"Go to the light? Sure, I can go to the light."

There was no more effort. No more struggle. Suddenly the smile on his face was magnificent. He was so happy, so excited.

"I'm in the light! I'm in the light!"

He started clapping his hands, patting himself on the shoulder, smiling broadly. The tubes in his arm didn't exist for him anymore as he reached out to shake hands with people I couldn't see, then clap his hands some more.

The joy on his face beautified my world, and I started clapping, too!

"Tom, what's happening?"

Nodding his head yes, he kept smiling.

"They're doing this!" Clapping, patting his shoulder, shaking hands in the air.

There he was clapping and smiling with new light in his eyes, and I was clapping and smiling with happy tears in mine.

"Tom, is everyone there?"

"Yes, everyone."

"Is Daddy there?"

"Yes!"

"And Nana?"

"Yes. And Big Bud!"

I didn't know who Big Bud was until my mother later reminded me that, in his very early childhood, Tom was called "Little Bud" by our Uncle Andy, whom Tom called "Big Bud." Just something between the two of them. Uncle Andy had passed away years ago.

"Tom, is God there?"

"Oh..." he seemed to glance around. "Probably."

Obviously, the seeming duality of Spirit and Matter, God and Man, was no longer Tom's concern. There was much more going on.

More clapping. Then a really big smile.

"Now they're getting ready. We're going to have a party for me—to celebrate."

He placed his hand on mine again.

"You're happy," I said.

"Oh, yes. I'm very happy."

"It's very beautiful there, isn't it?"

"It's *so* beautiful." He looked directly at me. "It's *extra special*."

He was very calm; his eyelids began to close. I began a litany of: "You're very happy. You're very safe. It's very beautiful."

Over and over. He would say yes, or nod his head, or simply smile.

Our mother arrived, and she witnessed what was taking place. She took my place at his bedside. He squeezed her hand.

About 20 minutes later, his body just didn't breathe anymore. Tom was now fully enjoying the party—his Celebration.

From Here to There

If you are with your loved one during the actual moments of passage from "here" to "there," you will know what to do. Have no concern about doing the "wrong" thing. With your love and compassion, nothing "wrong" can be done.

Remember that transformation is the loved one's process. It is the other person's show; you are an assistant. You need only be there, letting the person hold your hand if he wishes.

Do not think or presuppose that the person wants to die, doesn't want to die, that it is not time yet, or that it is past time. Your loved one is totally in charge now and will proceed with the process in the most appropriate way.

Just be there for this person. Let your loved one know you are there. Speak to him clearly, yet softly. If this person is a child, and if you are able, hold him on your lap, in your arms.

Do not try to hold this person's attention with words, but follow his lead. Tell your loved one often that he is safe. If you feel comfortable using the image of moving to the "light," then, by all means, verbally support him in his journey to that beautiful place. If doing so does not seem comfortable to you, then use reassuring words of safety, comfort, serenity, and peace.

If your loved one is in a coma, speak anyway. A part of the person *can* hear.

If being alone with your loved one is too much for you to endure, ask for support and assistance from a family member, a close friend, or from the hospital staff. You do not have to go through this experience alone.

Love the person who is dying. For the moment, go a step beyond yourself and the human level of experience that feels loss, that feels pain. Look beyond this person's form and feel the love that unifies all things. Know—tell yourself with assurance—that in this *true* love there can be no loss, no separation. There can be only love.

Breathe. Try to be aware of your breathing from time to time. Doing so will help still your mind and calm your thoughts.

When the Life Force of the loved one no longer needs to use the body as Its vehicle of expression here on earth, It will detach Itself, and the body will no longer breathe. With dignity, the soul has put the body to rest.

Do not call your loved one back. That Being is in the Divine Land now, safe from any worries and all harm.

Your loved one has awakened from a dream the rest of us still share. Allow the part of you that *knows* this...to rejoice.

The Witness

As a witness or assistant in a transformation process, remember that this process can be very tiring and draining for you. All of you—your body, mind, emotions, and Life Force—has been deeply involved in a death drama. Be aware that it is very natural and normal to feel exhausted and relieved at the same time. You may also be in shock.

Treat yourself well. Force yourself to do pleasant physical things immediately—a hot bath or Jacuzzi, a good meal, an hour of rest whether you sleep or not. The death process is over for the loved one, but not for you. It is very important for you to care about yourself now. This is a good time to use your personal journal or diary and write down:

— how you feel emotionally,
— what you are thinking, and
— how your body feels.

Write down everything and anything you would like to express.

The Other Side of Birth

When a baby is born, almost all parents feel a bit of anxiety about their infant's future. They may pray: "Dear God, don't let anything bad happen to my child."

When someone dies, there can be no anxiety for the person's future since the Life Force (God) can have no negative experiences. Know that those who die re-learn, or remember, the secrets of Life that they forgot at birth. So death, as the other side of birth, is remembering the glory of immortality.

Il n'y pas de morts.
(There are no dead.)

— Maurice Maeterlinck

When one dies, a chapter is not torn out of the book,
but translated into a better language.

— John Donne

We sometimes congratulate ourselves at the moment
of waking from a troubled dream; it may be so the
moment after death.

— Nathaniel Hawthorne

---

*I remember that my loved one
is a Child of the Universe.
I get out of the way.
The universe knows what to do.*

I am standing on the seashore. A ship spreads her sails to the morning breeze and starts for the ocean. I stand watching until she fades on the horizon, and someone at my side says, "She is gone!"

Gone where? The loss of sight is in me, not in her. Just at the moment when someone says, "She is gone," there are others who are watching her coming. Other voices take up the glad shout, "Here she comes!"

And that is dying.

— Anonymous

To die is landing on some distant shore.

— John Dryden

CHAPTER FOUR

After

Life Goes On, Death Doesn't

When the transition process is completed for your loved one, it is not over for you. The immediate stress and tension of being with the dying person is now replaced by a period of grief.

You may feel some relief that the process is now finished, and you may even say, "It's a blessing." However, a grieving time will most certainly follow the death of a loved one, and it can be harmful to deny yourself the time necessary to heal. The length of the mourning period will be different for each individual, but the time does pass, the heartache does diminish, the profound feelings of sadness do lift. *It just takes time.*

The beginning of healing is the shedding of your tears. Crying is the body's expression of release. Crying releases feelings of regret, anger, and pain. Crying is your body's acknowledgment of what you are experiencing and thinking; it enables you to get on the road to healing.

Give yourself permission to mourn.

As often as possible during the days immediately following a death, be aware of what is happening to you. Pay attention to your thoughts and feelings, and examine them. You don't have to change them, but be aware of what they are. Each day, in your personal journal or diary, write down the things you did or are going to do, how you feel, and what you're thinking. This process allows you to ease yourself back into your normal daily routine.

The Ceremonies

If you are involved in any of the varied religious or social ceremonies for the dead, appreciate them as symbols of your loved one's movement onto a higher plane.

You may wish to perform your own private ceremony or ritual in which, as a result of your love, you release this person to the new, more peaceful life he is now experiencing.

During any ceremony, it is important for you to be aware of your breathing. Although it is not necessary to constantly breathe deeply, it is a good idea to inhale and exhale completely—that is, complete each breath. Even remembering to do this occasionally will assist you in being clear in your thoughts and to maintain your sense of balance and stability.

It is not the great things you do that matter,
but the small things you do with great heart.

— Mother Teresa

Anger, Guilt, and Grief

Very often following a death, anger quickly rises from nowhere and strikes out against another person, thing, or situation. This is misdirected anger. We are *really* furious because a loved one died and left us.

This is a normal and natural step in our own healing process. Do not feel ashamed or embarrassed because you are angry. This emotion will dissipate with time and, in retrospect, you will understand why you felt as you did.

One of the best ways to release anger from your system is to pound some pillows with your fists. It may seem silly or meaningless at first, but it is the physical action of anger that helps to release the emotion of anger. You may also wish to record your feelings in your diary or journal, writing down just how angry you feel and why. These suggestions do not dignify or reinforce your anger; they help you get rid of it.

You may also experience a sense of guilt when a loved one passes away. This emotion may be very subtle and difficult to pinpoint, but it arises as a result of thinking you could have done something to change the outcome. Know that there is *nothing* you could have done! You are not responsible in any way for your loved one's death. That is a matter strictly between the person and the Universal Source of Life, or God. The feeling of guilt is just a little part of your inner makeup trying to convince you that you are a bad person. You are not. You are a good person.

It might help to select a piece of classical or soft music you especially enjoy and play it. Sit quietly, with your eyes closed, and imagine that the music flows into your toes and all the way up through your body, then out through your fingertips and out the top of your head. Each note of music cleanses you internally, and effortlessly eases any feelings that are not beneficial to you. Continue until the piece of music ends. You may wish to repeat the process.

There may be moments when you feel as though you will die from the sadness. You may think that the grief will never lift and the world will never again be bright for you. This is depression's "sledgehammer approach," and it is not at all subtle.

On a piece of paper or in your journal or diary, draw a picture of your heart—how it feels to you right now. You may want to color it. Then write down everything your heart is now feeling. When you're finished, draw another picture of how you *want* your heart to feel, and write down all the ways you want your heart to feel in the future. Then, write down five things you can do to help your heart feel better. This activity will help to motivate you; it will keep you from being mired in deep sadness for too long a time.

Magic Moments

When you make an effort to suppress your sadness, you're expending a great deal of energy in an attempt to deny an actual emotion. It's better to refocus on something other than your despondent feelings, thereby allowing these emotions to fade away naturally. Some suggestions for filling up the emptiness within you are to:

— take an exercise, dance, yoga, or Tai Chi class;
— read a spiritual book that will feed your soul;
— play a musical instrument, or listen to some music you find soothing;
— shop for something beautiful that will make you happy;
— watch a video or a TV program that will make you laugh;
— take yourself out for a good meal;
— engage in some form of athletic pursuit (walking, running, tennis, golf, etc.);
— visit a friend who is supportive and comforting, or invite friends over to visit you;
— take a drive somewhere that is close to nature (a park, a forest, a lake, etc.);
— visit an art gallery, or create a piece of art yourself;
— take a class in something that interests you;

— volunteer some of your time to a meaningful cause;
— spend some time around children and animals;
— join a bereavement support group; and/or
— garden, or pot new plants.

Studies show that having a pet in the house—a bird, fish, dog, cat, hamster, or any animal—naturally lessens the length of time and the intensity of the mourning period. Also, spending time in nature is both gratifying and healing. Go outside as often as you can. Air, sun, even rain and snow, can help you to heal. You will find that incorporating new activities into your day automatically helps to lessen your grief.

There may be subtle elements of depression that seem to overcome you when you least expect it. This state of mind does not have to be fought off; it can actually be recognized as small clouds that obscure the sun for a few moments.

Realize that you do not have the burdensome task of "picking up the pieces" of your life. You have the freedom to design new pieces of your life that fit perfectly.

Grief exists because you are human, and you have the ability to love others. Grief fades because you are human, and you have the ability to love others and to love yourself.

*Let the one who is sad, depressed, or unhappy find
some altruistic purpose into which he may pour his
whole being and he will find a new inflow of life of
which he has never dreamed.*

— from *The Science of Mind,* by Ernest Holmes

> *A tragedy can turn out to be our greatest good if we approach it in a way from which we can grow.*
>
> — Louise L. Hay

Movement

> *After Jose died, I made myself go back and forth down the walkway to the mailbox. A simple thing, but I had to make myself do it every day. Three years later I walked in my first marathon. It was just a local one for charity, but I walked a mile, and I was really smiling at the end.*
>
> — Lettie, age 75

Unhappiness has a special effect on the body. Sadness can bring a heaviness to the shoulders, a shuffle in the walk, even a bowing of the head. When in mourning, we may often desire the quietude of our own home, the comfort and safety of a favorite armchair. Quiet, comfort, and safety are all beneficial. However, holding grief in our bodies is not good. When muscles are tense, painful spasms can result; when muscles are not used, they will not be able to support or help oxygenate the skeletal frame.

You may not particularly feel like doing so right now, but it really is time to *move!* Walk around the room; take a stroll across the yard or around the block. You can move slowly and carefully, or you can run hard and fast. Do what you have enjoyed in the past: walk, swim, climb a hill, rollerskate, work out with weights, dance, and so on. There is no need to pretend to be joyful. It is simply time to move. It may help to affirm: "My body is my good friend, and I take care of it."

Your body is your first home here on Earth. It belongs only to you. Please do not allow bereavement to make it an unhealthy environment. You possess the gift of movement. Let it work for you. Move, breathe, help yourself heal.

> *I walk the dog for a half hour each day.*
> *That's the best I can do right now.*

— Marcus, recently widowed

> *What is life—*
> *It is the flash*
> *of a firefly*
> *in the night.*
> *It is the breath*
> *of a buffalo*
> *in the wintertime.*
> *It is the little shadow*
> *which runs along the grass*
> *and loses itself in the sunset.*

— Crowfoot

The Year That Follows

During the 12 months following the death of a loved one, there will be certain dates that will be significant to you, such as your loved one's birthday, or an anniversary, or a special day the two of you shared. Find a way to celebrate that day. Plan to do something that both expresses your love for the person who died and reinforces your own self-nurturing. If there is a burial site, you may wish to plant or take flowers there. These "special days" can carry with them a certain amount of stress, so it is important to be very good to yourself.

If you are experiencing anger or depression or just feeling that "something is wrong," it is a good idea to write a letter to the person who died. You can start by telling your loved one how you feel, then ask any questions you still may have regarding the person, events in his life, and even the transition itself. Conclude by telling your loved one what is happening in your life at the moment.

When you have finished and have read the letter over, you may burn it, tear it up, or keep it in your journal or diary for safekeeping.

Some people wish to wear a traditional symbol of mourning, such as a black armband or ribbon, for a period of time. This act of "wearing your emotion on your sleeve" makes it easier for other people to understand what you are going through. It can also aid in shortening the mourning period, because the symbol is a physical statement of sadness, and you will probably want to remove it sometime soon—a sign that you are healing.

Although the memory of your loved one is allowed to exist in all its intensity for whatever time you require, the first anniversary of the death can be marked with a Farewell Ceremony. This ceremony is of your own design and can be as simple as taking a walk or lighting candles in your home or place of worship. You may want to attend a church service. Whatever you decide, take this time to converse with the loved one in your imagination. Then gently, but firmly, let go. Let go.

Democracy of Death:
It comes equally to us all,
and makes us all equal when it comes.

— John Donne

Be the green grass above me,
With showers and dewdrops wet;
And if thou wilt, remember,
And if thou wilt, forget.

— Christina Rossetti

We cannot cure the world of sorrows, but we can
choose to live in joy.

— Joseph Campbell

I do not deceive myself by thinking I must suffer even though I feel this sense of loss. I remember that God loves me, and therefore, I love me, too.

And ye shall know the truth, and the truth shall make you free.

— John 8:32

Humanity shows itself in all its intellectual splendor during this age, as the sun shows itself at dawn....

— Maria Montessori

Set your presumptions aside about sickness and death, children and cancer. Prepare yourself for paradox. Where you suppose death to rule, life abounds. Where you expect pathos, there may be humor in its place. Children will lead and wise adults will follow. Leave your biases at the door.

— from *A Child Shall Lead Them,*
by Diane Komp, M.D.

CHAPTER
FIVE

The Death
of a Child

God, Patty, Me, and the Morning

by Patty's mom

I brought Patty home from the hospital that night because we all knew there would be no morning for her. I had gotten all the necessary hospital permission, and Patty was comfortable. As I held her in my arms in the rocking chair, I thought, Wouldn't it be nice if tomorrow morning just never came? If there was simply no tomorrow? A devastating earthquake or a nuclear war—and the morning just didn't come for any of us? That would be nice.

I rocked back and forth, holding my sleeping/dying daughter. She had just turned six: three years living and three years dying. I talked to her softly, as we rocked through each hour of the night. I told her everything, as she slept with heavy breathing. I talked to her about love and beauty and the special gifts she brought to me. When my voice cracked, I would rest my head back and try to breathe without shaking. It was at those times that I thought my own thoughts: How often did I cry so hard I would vomit? When did my husband and I really stop talking to each other? Did I still want desperately to kill God? Oh, how I so often wanted to kill God! I decided it wouldn't be necessary to kill God *if* something wonderful happened during this night, and there was no tomorrow morning. If we could all die with Patty, then I would let God live.

We rocked back and forth. Back and forth. I told my daughter about boys, and first grade, and the zoo. I quietly rambled on about things like ballet, water sports, and the Olympic Games.

At one point during the night, I began to actually somehow *feel* that I was holding less and less of "her" to my heart. I rocked and cried and held her tighter.

Sometime later we just stopped rocking. In my head, I could hear Patty telling me that "rocking is for babies," and "I'm a big girl now." I carried her to the couch, brushed back her hair, and covered her with a new Snoopy blanket—one she hadn't seen before. I held her hand.

"I'm a big girl now." I had to chuckle at the memory of a hospital visit last week (was it only last week?), when I arrived to find Patty and her little wing-mates all done up in lipstick, blush, and eyeshadow—playing "big girls" and giggling themselves silly!

I'm sure Patty knew I was thinking about this, because she smiled. Her eyes were closed, but she really smiled. And not a baby smile either. It was a warm, adult, loving smile, filled with wisdom. My Patty was a big girl now. She was such a big girl that she let go of my hand.

I made the necessary phone calls. And I told God I changed my mind. Now that Patty was safe in another world, I needed the morning to arrive in this world, and I needed it very badly.

Even though I cried a lot, what was most important was that I could—and still can—see her beautiful, ageless, smile-of-wisdom and hear Patty's voice in my head saying: "I'm a big girl now."

And as it has, and will, morning came.

A Child Is Dying

A child is terminally ill and is going to die. It simply makes no sense. It makes no sense at all. Please know that it also makes no sense to doctors, nurses, parents, and families throughout the world. Although this is a painfully unique experience for you, you are not alone when your child is dying.

All the questions can be answered and resolved, or unanswered and forgotten, in the years to come. Right now, you are in a special time, the most special time in your child's life, no matter how long you have been together. It is so hard. And it hurts.

There is nothing in the world that holds greater promise than a young life. And when that young life is leaving *your* life, the sadness and grief may seem at times overwhelming and all-consuming. Although it may seem unbearable, it is necessary now to maintain a sense of right action, or normalcy, in your daily life. Yes, your thoughts and love are centered on your child, yet it is important not to neglect Life itself. Communicate your thoughts and feelings to family members and special friends. It is not a time to shut out other loved ones. You may think that no one could ever understand the pain you're feeling; however, people will try to understand and support you if you will let them.

During this critical time, ask and allow others to do things for you: grocery shop, clean the house, babysit other children, and so on. You are going through a very demanding time and will benefit by turning some tasks over to others. The Universe is a strong and steady support system. Accept help now.

As is the case with the impending death of any loved one, it is essential for you to take some time to nurture yourself. A warm bath, a walk in nature, a good dinner, even an exercise class, is not running away from your child. It is helping you lessen the stress of the days so you will be better equipped emotionally to spend time with your child. Even as you buy toys, games, books to bring to the hospital or sick room, try to buy a little something for yourself.

These things may sound so unimportant as you face the passing of a very special part of you. However, using some physical energy to nurture yourself acknowledges that *you* exist and fortifies your own well-being. Doing little things for yourself enables you to cope. And, please, try to remember to breathe. Several times a day, sit or stand and breathe deeply and evenly.

If your child is in a hospital or hospice, speak to the doctors and nurses. Ask any questions regarding your child that come to mind. Do not hesitate to make suggestions regarding your child's comfort. The staff is there to assist patients and parents. And, although your child is his own authority in the transformation process, you are the adult in charge of life proceedings.

By all means, touch your child. We are all soothed by loving touch. Even if your child is asleep or in a coma, hold him in your arms, sing and talk softly to your child, this wonderful individual expression of an Infinite Universe.

No matter how old your child is, gently massage his hands, feet, and back. Touching is reassuring love. Make your child as comfortable as possible, and enliven the environment with colorful objects—pictures, toys, plants—things that your son's or daughter's eyes enjoy seeing.

If your child is old enough to talk, please listen. Allow him the freedom to express thoughts, feelings, even fears. Answer questions as honestly as you can. Laugh with the child, and smile, smile, smile—with all the love in your heart.

If your child is asking you about sickness and death and you just *cannot* bear to engage in that conversation, please ask for help from personnel, clergy, or counselors trained in death education. You are very busy during this time, yet you may want to accept the assistance of a counselor for yourself and perhaps the entire family. A professional listener (therapist, psychologist, practitioner) for you to talk to—someone who is not personally involved in your daily life—can be a blessing at this time. *You do not have to be alone at this time!*

However, when you are by yourself, there are productive things you can do. You can cry. You can feel the emotions as they seem to sweep over you. You can write down what you're feeling by using words, images, colors in your journal or diary. You can let it all out!

In death, the body and soul lovingly release each other for the continual progression of that special expression, or aspect, of God whom you know as your child. You too need to release, as often as necessary, the feelings of pain, loss, confusion, even hatred, that you may be experiencing. Putting it all in a journal, which you may either keep or later destroy, helps you release these feelings and assists you in beginning to heal the rest of your life.

You can also see your child in your mind, enveloped and surrounded by a bright, protective light. Sit comfortably at home, in the park, at the ocean, or in the room where your child sleeps, and close your eyes. Mentally picture your child enfolded in the color of joy. Turn your attention away from your immediate feelings, and focus all your thoughts on the beautiful image of your child in total safety and perfect joy.

At another time, sit quietly and imagine the Universe (or God) as a huge, never-ending, brilliantly cut diamond. See all the millions, even trillions, of shining facets in this perfect Whole. All of your family members, friends, and even strangers comprise their own shining facet. Each is a part of the whole. So is your child a magnificent part of the Whole, part of the Universe, part of God. And, just as none of the shining facets can ever be lost or missing or tarnished, neither can your child's life ever really end. The experience of life on Earth may diminish and fade, yet Spirit-as-your-child continues forever as part of the Whole.

Just as you are, your child is a manifestation of Infinite Good here on Earth. Although Infinite Good can change appearances, change forms, It can never die. The Infinite Universe holds you and your child, as you hold each other, in Its heart forever.

If it is possible, hold your child in your arms as he makes the final journey to a better life. Even if he is just an infant, talk to your child, ease the life with words and touch through the short space of grayness into the light.

You have already been proclaimed a very special person, since this child of Spirit had chosen you as Its parent here on Earth. Whatever you do to assist the child in returning to a greater Home, in awakening from the Earth dream, is perfect.

When it is over, know that your child shines in the Mind of God, which is your Mind, also. Lay your child's form to rest with the special dignity and love that your son or daughter deserves.

I thank life for sharing this child with me.
We both loved well in the time we had together.

Sudden Infant Death

by Kate's mom

My son is married now, and I'm about to be a grandmother. My daughter is in graduate school. My husband and I are doing well; we are healthy and happy. I keep saying "My, My, My"—I sound so possessive! I think that's because you asked me to tell you about Kate—"My Kate."

My Kate, my firstborn, my baby. I was 21 years old, and what a joy! Married to the man I loved since high school and the mother of a beautiful baby. She was such a good baby—healthy, smiling, kicking, and she hardly ever cried. I loved to look at her so much that I would check on her four or five times a night just to see her and smile.

It was on a Thursday night, or rather, early Friday morning, that I went in to check on her, and she was dead. Just like that. My Kate was not there anymore. A lifeless wax doll had taken her place. "My" baby was dead, and she didn't even say goodbye.

It's not hard to remember. I cried and I hated. I hated myself, I hated my husband, I hated every baby I saw—even the ones on television commercials. It took time. I tried to love the memory of Kate, but after I stopped thinking: How could I have done this to my baby?, I started thinking: How could my baby have done this to me? It was hard, and it was over 25 years ago.

I had to learn to love and accept love again. I had to learn to release Kate and still keep her in my heart. I had to learn to stop "blaming" myself and Kate. I had to learn that my identity is *me* and not "the mother of."

I still think of Kate, and it's funny, but throughout the years she has—sort of—grown with me. She never stopped being a part of my life because she *was* an important part of my life.

The most important thing I learned is that love never stops. Oh, I know, for a while after Kate was gone I didn't feel much love....

If it were possible, I would put my arms around every mother and father who has suffered a crib death. I would hold them tight and let them cry. I would tell them that the love never really stops and...although I don't know how or when this happens...life does become good again. They will wake up one morning, and the memory of their baby will *not* be the first thing on their minds. I would promise them this. I know it is the truth.

Missing Children

If I could only know for certain that Mike was dead.
He has been missing for two years. He would be 14
now. I try to tell myself that he's dead so I can start
to grieve for him. I even tried to go back coaching
Little League this year, but driving to the school,
I broke down and cried...again.

— Mike's dad

Where are they? Those little faces we see all around us these days under the words *Missing* and *Have you seen me?* Where are they? And why aren't they home?

The grief that surrounds the family of a missing child is felt by their friends, loved ones, and even strangers in the community. It is also a double bind: we feel the anguish of the loss, but is mourning premature?

Please know that you are not willing your child dead by experiencing grief over his disappearance. You are keeping hope alive by mourning for yourself. So, do all you think is necessary to keep *your* life going. Be in contact with the authorities and members of the community. This is not a time to hide your feelings, even your rage. Talk to people. If your voice is shaky, let it be heard anyway. You, and how you feel, are very important.

A missing child is not a quiet grief. It is an outrage reaching epidemic proportions in the United States. By communicating (telling family, friends, police, civil authorities, other parents, children, the clergy, and so on, how you feel) you are helping to alter the mass consciousness of a society where "children are missing every day."

However, with love and compassion, you are urged caution. Do *not* take the law into your own hands. Doing so could be very harmful. Know that there is, within each of us and your child, a greater Law of Life in which nothing is ever lost or missing.

Use this Law for you and your child. Whenever—and every time—you see your child in your mind, surround him with the strongest, brightest light possible. This is not game playing; this is consciously focusing your attention on life and light. Replace all the images of terror in your mind with the strong image of your child in the light of love. Include yourself in this light with your child.

Use a personal, private journal or diary to put in writing how you feel. No one need ever read it but you. You can later burn the entries if you wish, but be assured that writing releases much emotion, confusion, and fear. It helps to ease the pain.

Write letters in your journal to your child. Write many letters. Tell your child what you are feeling. Ask him questions. Tell him that you are sending out love and protection from your heart and that you truly desire his return home.

Join with other parents who are experiencing this same profound sadness. Even if there are moments when you feel that gathering in this way is pointless, please know that by spending time with others you are adding a balance to your life that is much needed now.

Try to take care of yourself. Allow the waves of fear and emptiness to roll over you and fade away. Breathe. Whenever you think of it, stand still and breathe.

Reinforce your knowledge, even if you don't feel you "believe" it, that your child is safe in a Universe of protection and love. Focus your attention on love and trust.

Mourning the Loss of a Child

Sadness	Hostility
Low self-esteem	Hysteria
Hyperactivity	Nightmares
Mis/noncommunication	Confusion
Irritability	Indecision
Inadequacy	Depression

If you are the parent of a child who has died, the above list may define some of your present feelings and actions. You are not going mad, crazy, or insane. You are mourning the passing of a young one.

Somewhere inside, you feel you gave birth to a baby to care for and love. The child, at whatever age, died before you did—and that was not what you expected of life. For reasons that seem unknowable right now, you have been dealt a nasty blow.

Grieve. It was not "just a child," and grief can never be measured by the size/weight/age of the one who moved on. And you will not "just get over it" because you will now spend time working to live beyond it.

As you stand in your child's room and see the furnishings, toys, clothes, and special things, close your eyes and place your hand on your heart. Feel it beating. Feel the life that flows through you. Just stand quietly and feel your own heartbeat. Know that you are a living child of the Universe, and although this time may be very difficult for you, your heart will beat as the days pass. You will survive.

It may be very therapeutic and rewarding for you to donate your child's toys and other belongings to a children's home or to the children's wing at a hospital or hospice. In this way, the energy of your child's possessions is passed on to other children. A part of him continues to brighten the lives of others.

It is very important, now, that you do not build a wall around yourself. Talk to your family and friends. You may wish to have some regular sessions with a therapist trained in mourning counseling.

Take time for yourself. You will not forget your child, neither will you hold on to the pain of the child's absence. When you do not mask your mourning, you will not dwell on it.

(Please incorporate the suggestions in Chapter 4 to help you move through and beyond the present sadness.)

Mourning heals. Love yourself and allow it to happen. You show love and respect for your child when you continue to live your life, to let the days unfold as they will.

The Universe loves you. God loves you. And so it is.

Peace I leave with you; my peace I give to you....
Let not your hearts be troubled.

— John 14:27

Little Child, Big Soul

Know that this child is not a "poor little soul." This child is a resplendent acknowledgment of Life that can never die. The soul of a child is neither poor nor little. It is large, loving, beautiful, and healthy, just as the Source Itself.

The child came to teach and to learn. And, although it may have happened too quickly for you, the child has completed his mission. He can now move on to even greater expressions of life and love. You and I have more to teach and more to learn.

Bless the child who graduates ahead of us. Even if in tears, bless the child who finished his mission before the rest of us finished ours. Take heart that you have loved and been loved by a very special aspect of God. Your child is always a precious part of Infinite Life, and so are you.

Rest, and be assured.

Today I carefully release any thoughts
that God "took" my child. God gives,
and my child accepts, a new and glorious
morning.

...for you must go
and I must die.
But come ye back
when summer's in the meadow
or when the valley's hushed
and white with snow.
For I'll be here
in sunshine and in shadow.
Oh Danny boy
I love you so.

— Irish Folksong

CHAPTER SIX

Death in a Child's Life

For the Children

I was three years old when my grandmother died, and I still remember two things about that time:

> — I got to wear my new burgundy snowsuit when I stopped at the wake for a moment with my mom.

> — I couldn't figure something out—Nana went to heaven to be happy with God, so why was everybody so sad?

The death of a family member, friend, or pet in a child's experience can be devastating or, as it was in my case, quite confusing.

Be aware of, and understand, your own feelings first, and be willing to let your child know how you feel. Your child learns from you that emotions of sadness and feelings of loss are okay right now and that they will pass.

Hold your child as he's experiencing moments of grief. Physical contact heals.

Tell your child the truth when questions are asked. If some questions are unanswerable ("But *why* did Grandpa die?"), tell your son or daughter that you just don't know—

that only God knows—but explain that the question is a good one to ask and a hard one to answer.

You will want to encourage your child to express, as often as needed, how he is feeling about death. Be sure your child is not blaming himself for causing the death. ("I was bad, so Grandpa left me.")

Remember that anger is a part of grief—yours and your child's—and direct that anger into pillow pounding and discussions. This is also an excellent time for the child, if he is old enough, to use a journal or diary to record thoughts and feelings.

The best way to *not* reinforce fear in the child is, first, to be open and honest about thoughts and feelings; second, to provide security for your child by explaining that no one was to blame and that no one could have changed the outcome; and third, by teaching the child that the Life Force (or whatever term you prefer) of the person never really dies and always continues to love him. And don't forget: concentrate on life. Do some "favorite things" or new activities with your child.

My four-year-old friend, Yves, experienced the death of his kitten. He and his mother had a burial ceremony for the cat, and they discussed at length what death was all about. His mother was very careful to explain that it is okay to cry and feel sad for a while. She held him, answered all his questions, encouraged him to express how he felt and what he was thinking. That afternoon, she took him shopping. In the toy store, he let out a big sigh and said quietly to himself, "Oh, Kitty!"

That instant was his healing. By nightfall, his grief had passed, and Yves was on the phone with me, telling me the story of Kitty—how she had died, and that he had been very sad, but now he felt pretty good because he knew that Kitty was just "playing somewhere else."

Look to the children, not away from them. Be honest and fair. As you comfort them, know that they are comforting you, too.

The Rainbow Bridge

> There is a bridge connecting Heaven and Earth. It is called the Rainbow Bridge because of its many colors. Just this side of the Rainbow Bridge there is a land of meadows, hills, and valleys with lush green grass.
>
> When a beloved pet dies, the pet goes to this place. There is always food and water and warm spring weather. The old and frail animals are young again. Those who are maimed are made whole again. They play all day with each other.
>
> There is only one thing missing. They are not with their special person who loved them on Earth. So, each day they run and play until the day comes when one suddenly stops playing and looks up! The nose twitches! The ears are up! The eyes are staring! And this one suddenly runs from the group!
>
> You have been seen, and when you and your special friend meet, you take him or her in your arms and embrace. Your face is kissed again and again and again, and you look once more into the eyes of your trusting pet.
>
> Then you cross the Rainbow Bridge together, never again to be separated.
>
> — Author unknown

Today I practice Love. I begin to heal as I remember to forgive.

The brevity of life, which is so constantly
lamented, may be the best quality it possesses.

— Arthur Schopenhauer

His dog up and died,
Up and died.
After twenty years,
He still grieved.

— "Mr. Bojangles"
by Jerry Jeff Walker

CHAPTER SEVEN

The Death of a Pet

Our Best Friends

I raised Max from a 10-day-old, 5½-ounce kitten. He died at age 2, weighing 17 pounds. I was heartbroken. For the longest time, I would turn and see him—but he really wasn't there.

The loss of an animal in one's life can carry with it the same feelings as the loss of a beloved friend or relative.

Since everything that lives is composed of energy, and energy can only be transformed, not destroyed, know that the energy or Life Force of the animal still exists, although its form does not.

Pets are our own reflections. They are dearly attuned to us, and we to them.

If your pet must be put to sleep in a veterinarian's office, try to stay with the animal. Stroke it, talk to it, ease it from "here" to "there." If your pet is not in pain but is fading at home, make it comfortable, warm, and provide plenty of water. It is not necessary to sit by the animal constantly, but don't ignore it either. Talk to the pet in a clear, gentle voice. Speak to it in your mind, as well. Avoid loud noises, and don't disturb your pet by waking it.

Sit quietly and close your eyes. Select a color that represents to you warmth, safety, comfort, and peace. Imagine that you can cover the animal completely in this color. When you see it totally enveloped in this color, tell your pet in your mind that it is safe and peaceful. Love your pet in your thoughts. When it feels comfortable to you, open your eyes.

After the animal is gone, you may want to have a private or family ceremony in which, with love, you release your pet's energy to its home in the Universe. Thank your pet for sharing its life with you.

In your journal or diary, write a letter to your animal. Tell your pet everything you want to say: how you feel, how much you miss your pet, that you feel sad, angry, and so on. This process is also a good idea for children to do when a pet has died.

Chances are that you will find yourself mourning your pet with many of the same feelings that you would have when a human being has passed away. It is beneficial to acknowledge and explore these feelings, just as it is very therapeutic to weep over the loss of your pet.

Allowing the feelings "out" enables them to fade faster.

By all means, when you feel comfortable with the idea, definitely adopt a new pet. Love brings more love, and there are many animals needing homes who are ready and willing to give you an abundance of love!

God never abandons Its creations;
therefore, I know my pet is safe at Home.

*To fear death, gentlemen, is nothing other than
to think oneself wise when one is not; for it is
to think one knows what one does not know.
No man knows whether death may not even
turn out to be the greatest of blessings for a
human being: and yet people fear it as if they
knew for certain that it is the greatest of evils.*

— Socrates

*All of us loved him very much. With trust in
God, we all pray that David has finally found
the peace that he did not find in life.*

— Senator Edward Kennedy, after the suicide
of his 29-year-old nephew, David

*When we "die," my guides said, we experience
nothing more than a transition to another state. Our
spirits slip from the body to a more spiritual realm. If
our deaths are traumatic, the spirit quickly leaves the
body, sometimes even before death occurs. If a person
is in an accident or fire, for example, their spirit may
be taken from their body before they experience pain.
The body may actually appear still alive for some
moments, but the spirit will have already left and be in
a state of peace.*

— from *Embraced by the Light,* by Betty J. Eadie

Sudden Death

Shock

When a loved one has died suddenly—in an accident, a war, as the result of suicide, or as the victim of a violent crime—the pain and confusion you feel is often heightened because you are truly in shock.

It is very important to immediately start taking special care of yourself. Rest as much as possible, even if you don't sleep. Eat nourishing foods. Take warm baths. Allow your body to start releasing the shock and stress *first*. Then you can begin to handle all your other thoughts and emotions more clearly.

During the first few days following a sudden death, take five or ten minutes every two hours to sit or stand quietly and breathe deeply. Gently fill your lungs with air, then slowly exhale. Do this slowly, over and over again.

In a sudden-death situation, very often thoughts arise such as:

"If I had said _____, this wouldn't have happened."
"If I had done _____, this wouldn't have happened."

You must understand that you had *nothing* to do with your loved one's death. ***No one dies unless the Life Force (soul) of that person agrees to leave the planet.*** You may not ever fully understand the reason for this person's transition right now, but be assured that you need not blame yourself for another soul's decision to leave the planet.

In your journal or diary, imagine that you are having a conversation with the person who has died, and write it out just as you would a script for a play. Write down a question, and then write down what the person "says" in response. Continue until the written conversation comes to a natural ending. You may repeat this process over and over.

You may also wish to write your loved one a letter asking all the unanswered questions you have on your mind. By putting the questions down in writing, you are helping to clear your inner confusion.

Throughout your mourning period, just remember to take very good care of yourself. Use the suggestions in Chapter 4 to help you deal daily with grief. Be willing to seek professional assistance—a therapist or counselor trained to help those in mourning. Most important, know (and you already *do* know this somewhere within you) that the person who made a transformation is safe and secure, free from pain, worry, and fear.

The grief surrounding you will lift. In time, it will be gone. One day—soon—you will feel the sun rising in your heart again.

I know it. So do you.

I give myself the gift of resting
for just one moment, in the peace
of knowing that God is all there is.

Then is it sin
To rush into the secret house of death
Ere death dare come to us?

— from *Antony and Cleopatra,*
by William Shakespeare

Suicide/Homicide

The shock comes first. The unthinkable, the unbelievable has happened to you. The rage, the horrifying anger is equaled only by an intensely sad heartsickness. It is tragic. It is time to cry, to wail, to pound the wall with your fists. There can be no denial. A beautiful loved one is suddenly no longer here on this Earth. Someone has taken his life, or he has taken his own. This is a devastating, unplanned occurrence over which you had no control.

Throughout the first shock period following a suicide or homicide, your concentration will most likely be on your deep and, perhaps, conflicting emotions. Let these emotions exist with respect. Time will pass, and these emotions will change.

Some strong, loving words of caution: this is not the time to do anything harmful to anyone or anything. Seeking revenge is not how the Universe or Spirit or God works. Feelings of anger, even hatred, are legitimate emotions right now. Yet, do not, please do not, defile the goodness of your loved one by acting out these emotions.

You are not the judge in this circumstance. What happened is *truly* between the person or people involved and God. Start to slowly and carefully take yourself out of the scenario of this unexpected death. You are not the person who passed away, and you are not the totality of God.

Let this idea begin to be a comfort to you: none of us ever completely knows all that is in the heart and mind of another. Each person is a facet of the Magnificent, linked to It by his own extremely individual and personal thread. Each and every being has a unique communication with God that goes far beyond our mortal imaginations when the person reaches the Infinite.

Treat yourself kindly. Here on Earth we do not have a true, full understanding of so many confusing, heartbreaking events. Yet no soul dies; each soul grows in strength, wisdom, and love. Your precious loved one is not being judged by a vengeful God. The soul of your friend quickens with love now, perhaps resting for a time in the comforting arms of Light.

You need to rest, also. Rest your body. Even fitful sleep helps calm a troubled mind. Allow family, friends, and neighbors to assist you with tasks, and give yourself some quiet, peaceful time to aid your healing process.

Soon it will be time to talk to understanding people and verbally begin to release the pain you have inside. Taking the time for qualified counseling will assist you greatly. You may also wish to enlist the aid of a Victims of Crime or suicide support group in your area.

In time you will remember that Infinite Love is all-inclusive, and no one, no matter what, is ever left out or shunned or forgotten. Love the one who is no longer with you, and let God do the rest.

He who does not accept and respect those who
want to reject life, does not truly accept and respect
life itself.

— Thomas Szasz

Collective Consciousness and the Death of Strangers

*The crew of the space shuttle Challenger honored us
by the manner in which they lived their lives. We will
never forget them, nor the last time we saw them this
morning as they prepared for their journey and
waved goodbye and 'slipped the surly bonds of Earth
to touch the face of God.'*

— President Ronald Reagan

On January 28, 1986, the American space vehicle Challenger exploded upon take-off from Earth. Seven astronauts—seven vital, active men and women, died in the blast that shook the clouds.

Yet, the shock of it was not just that they died, it is that—quite simply, in the blink of an eye—they no longer existed. They vanished. There was nothing left. And we saw it all on television.

Immediate, visual access to death is part of our lives now. We no longer wait to read the newspaper for accounts of accidents, wars, or other types of devastation. We just turn on television and view it all. The Vietnam War, the Gulf War, the conflict in Bosnia—we've graphically seen death live and in color. Car accidents, violent crimes, bombings, hostage situations, the aftermaths of hurricanes, earthquakes, and tornadoes—they're all videoed by someone and delivered directly to us via electronic media.

The effects of the "death of strangers" is perhaps more subtle than the passing of a loved one who is close to us, yet it is a loss we feel either consciously or subconsciously, and it is something to be acknowledged.

When you read or hear or see the deaths of others in accidents, wars, or natural disasters, how do you feel? You certainly need not dwell on the catastrophe, but take a moment. Feelings of compassion, confusion, sadness, and even hurt are very real to us when we experience, even via television, the death of others.

After the Oklahoma City bombing
on April 19, 1995:

For the past two weeks, tears have come to my eyes, and my throat closes tight whenever I look at my five-year-old twin grandsons. Each night I ask God, "Who could bomb babies playing in a daycare center?" Each night God answers me and says, "Rest now, Edna. I will take care of it. I will take care of it all."

— Edna, age 64

My friend Marcie and I put real cute clothes on two of our tiny dolls. Then we dug a hole in the backyard with spoons and buried the dolls. We wanted the little kids who just died to have some dolls in heaven. My Momma asked our neighbor if she could cut some pansies from their garden to put on their graves. The neighbor said yes. And then she and Momma were crying. The flowers looked real nice.

— Yolanda, age 8

I'm a Vietnam vet. I couldn't imagine anything that would ever again make me feel sick, sad, and angry all at the same time. Now I see all the flags at half-mast, and I pray to God to help the folks in Oklahoma City and to help me.

— Martin, age 50

There is only one Infinite Intelligence, and we are *all* a part of that same Thing, or Life Force. Since all human beings can communicate with each other (in words, sign language, movement, music, eye contact, and in thought), are we not, then, responsible for what we communicate?

Race Mind, or mass thinking (thinking the way everybody around us thinks), is very tricky. It takes a bit of "thought" to release ourselves from it. We have all, at one time or another, held a belief that was a result of thinking along with the masses. Such simple thoughts as "I get the flu every winter; everyone does," or "The economy is rotten, so we'll never have enough money," or "Being overweight runs in my family," or even the basic "Blue is for boys, pink is for girls," are examples of mass thinking.

By taking responsibility for how we individually think, we can change our own thoughts and life experiences. Since there is only one Infinite Intelligence, and because we are all part of It, when we change our own thoughts to the positive, we are helping to change the thinking of an entire race.

Think for a moment about how you used to feel about the subject of death and dying. Is it possible now to accept the possibility that life always continues? What do you think the prevailing Race Mind opinion is about death? Does the human race generally think that death is the end of everything? The cruelest cut of all?

Now, what makes you *feel* better, way deep inside: knowing that death is the end of existence, or knowing that the energy of life is eternal?

I do not deny the emotions involved in the loss of a loved one or a stranger. However, I do support our knowing that the word *death* is just a short term for transformation or graduation from days spent on Earth to the next better experience.

When a catastrophe occurs, there is a natural "collective mourning"—a national or international connectedness, as we all express sorrow and grief for the victims. Now is the time to watch your thoughts. Now is the time to *know* in your mind and your heart that those who no longer live on Earth have simply gone before us. They do not have more to learn or more to teach here. *We do!*

Infinite Love extends
beyond the Universe,
extends beyond death.

Poem for the Living

When I am dead
Pray for me a little,
Think of me sometimes,
But not too much.
It is not good for you
To allow your thoughts to dwell
Too long on the dead.
Think of me now and again
As I was in life.
At some moment that is pleasant to recall.
But not for long.
Leave me in peace
As I shall leave you, too, in peace.
While you live
Let your thoughts be with the living.

— Anonymous

Recommended Reading

General:

Aries, Philip, THE HOUR OF DEATH. Vintage Books, 1982.

Coughlin, Ruth, GRIEVING: A LOVE STORY. Harper Collins, 1993.

Dean, Amy E., FACING LIFE'S CHALLENGES: Daily Meditations for Overcoming Depression, Grief, and "The Blues." Hay House, 1995.

de Beauvoir, Simone, A VERY EASY DEATH. Warner Paperback Library, 1973.

Donnelley, Nina Herrman, I NEVER KNOW WHAT TO SAY. Ballantine Books, 1987.

Ericsson, Stephanie, COMPANION THROUGH THE DARKNESS: Inner Dialogues on Grief. Harper Collins, 1993.

Hay, Louise L., LIFE! Reflections on Your Journey. Hay House, 1995.

_____, YOU CAN HEAL YOUR LIFE. Hay House, 1985.

Kennedy, Alexandra, LOSING A PARENT: Passage to a New Way of Living. Harper Collins, 1991.

Kübler-Ross, Elisabeth, ON DEATH AND DYING. MacMillan, 1969.

_____, ON LIFE AFTER DEATH. Celestial Arts, 1991.

Levang, Elizabeth and Ilse, Sherokee, REMEMBERING WITH LOVE: Messages of Hope for the First Year of Grieving and Beyond. Deaconess Press, 1992.

Levine, Stephen, WHO DIES? An Investigation of Conscious Living and Conscious Dying. Doubleday, 1982.

_____, MEETINGS AT THE EDGE. Doubleday, 1984.

Lewis, C.S., A GRIEF OBSERVED. Harper Collins, 1989.

Martin, Reverend John D., I CAN'T STOP CRYING. Key Porter Books (Canada), 1992.

Moffat, Mary Jane, IN THE MIDST OF WINTER: Selections from the Literature of Mourning. Vintage Books, 1982.

Moody, Raymond A., LIFE AFTER LIFE. Bantam, 1976.

Mumford, Amy Ross, IT HURTS TO LOSE A SPECIAL PERSON. Accent Expressions, 1982.

Nuland, Sherman B., HOW WE DIE. Alfred E. Knopf, 1994.

Osis, Karlis, and Haraldsson, Erlendur, AT THE HOUR OF DEATH. Avon Books, 1977.

Price, Eugenia, GETTING THROUGH THE NIGHT: Finding Your Way After the Death of a Loved One. Dial Press, 1982.

Quill, Thomas E., DEATH AND DIGNITY. W.W. Norton and Co., 1993

Rando, Theresa A., HOW TO GO ON LIVING WHEN SOMEONE YOU LOVE DIES. Bantam Books, 1991.

_____, LOSS AND ANTICIPATORY GRIEF. Lexington Books, 1986.

Rapoport, Nessa, A WOMAN'S BOOK OF GRIEVING. William Morrow and Co., 1994.

Reed, Paul, SERENITY. Celestial Arts, 1990.

Roth, Deborah, and LeVier, Emily, BEING HUMAN IN THE FACE OF DEATH. IBS Press, 1990.

Staudacher, Carol, MEN AND GRIEF. New Harbinger Publications, 1991.

Temes, Roberta, LIVING WITH AN EMPTY CHAIR: A Guide Through Grief. Irvington Publishers, 1984.

Whitmore, Martha Hickman, HEALING AFTER LOSS: Daily Meditations for Working Through Grief. Avon Books, 1994.

Loss of a Spouse:

Curry, Cathleen L., WHEN YOUR SPOUSE DIES. Ave Maria Press, 1990.

DiGiulio, Robert C., BEYOND WIDOWHOOD: From Bereavement to Emergence and Hope. MacMillan, 1989.

Feinberg, Linda, I'M GRIEVING AS FAST AS I CAN: How Young Widows and Widowers Can Cope and Heal. New Horizon Press. 1994.

Garrison, Gene K., WIDOW OR WIDOW TO BE? Coping with Change. Burning Gate Press, 1991.

Truman, Jill, LETTER TO MY HUSBAND. Viking Penguin, 1987.

Children:

Barbanell, Sylvia, WHEN A CHILD DIES. Pilgrims Book Services, 1984.

Buscaglia, Leo, THE FALL OF FREDDY THE LEAF. Holt, Reinhart and Winston, 1982.

Donnelly, Katherine Fair, RECOVERING FROM THE LOSS OF A CHILD. MacMillan, 1982.

Grollman, Earl A., TALKING ABOUT DEATH: Dialogue Between Parent and Child. Beacon Press, 1990.

Juneau, Barbara Frisbie, SAD BUT O.K. MY DADDY DIED TODAY: A Child's View of Death. Blue Dolphin Publishing, 1988.

Komp, Diane, A CHILD SHALL LEAD THEM. Zondervan Publishing House, 1993.

Kübler-Ross, Elisabeth, ON CHILDREN AND DEATH. MacMillan, 1980.

Leon, Irving G., WHEN A BABY DIES. Yale University Press, 1990.

Mumford, Amy Ross; and Danhauer, Karen E., LOVE AWAY MY HURT: A Child's Book About Death. Accent Expressions, 1983.

Rofes, Eric E., and The Unit at Fayerweather Street School, THE KIDS BOOK ABOUT DEATH AND DYING. Little, Brown and Co., 1985.

Aids:

Brown, Marie Annette and Powell-Cope, Gail M., CARING FOR A LOVED ONE WITH AIDS. University of Washington Press, 1994.

Donnelly, Katherine Fair, RECOVERING FROM THE LOSS OF A LOVED ONE WITH AIDS. St. Martin's Press, 1994.

Eidson, Ted (ed.), THE AIDS CAREGIVERS HANDBOOK. St. Martin's Press, 1993.

Hay, Louise L., THE AIDS BOOK: Creating a Positive Approach. Hay House, 1988.

Kübler-Ross, Elisabeth, AIDS: THE ULTIMATE CHALLENGE. MacMillan, 1993.

Near-Death Experiences:

Atwater, P.M.H., BEYOND THE LIGHT: What Isn't Being Said About Near Death Experience. Birch Lane Press, 1994.

Brinkley, Dannion, SAVED BY THE LIGHT. Random House, 1994.

Browne, Mary T., REFLECTIONS ON THE OTHER SIDE. Ballantine Books, 1994.

Eadie, Betty J., EMBRACED BY THE LIGHT. Bantam Books, 1994.

Moody, Raymond A., COMING BACK. Bantam Books, 1990.

Suicide / Homicide:

Donnelly, John (ed.), SUICIDE: RIGHT OR WRONG? Prometheus Books, 1990.

Lukas, Christopher and Seiden, Henry M., SILENT GRIEF: Living in the Wake of a Suicide. Bantam Books, 1987.

Quinnett, Paul G., SUICIDE: THE FOREVER DECISION. Crossroad Publishing Co., 1993.

Wrobleski, Adina, SUICIDE: SURVIVORS—A Guide for Those Left Behind. Afterwood Publishing, 1991.

Right to Die / Assisted Deaths:

Hill, Patrick T., and Shirley, David, A GOOD DEATH. Choice in Dying Inc./The National Council for the Right to Die, 1992.

Humphry, Derek, FINAL EXIT. Dell Publishing, 1992.

Pets:

Nieburg, Herbert A., and Fischer, Arlene, PET LOSS: A Thoughtful Guide for Parents and Children. Harper and Row, 1982.

Pitcairn Richard H., "Saying Goodbye: Coping with a Pet's Death" from DR.PITCAIRN'S COMPLETE GUIDE TO NATURAL HEALTH FOR DOGS AND CATS. Rodale Press, 1982.

The Monks of New Skete, "Facing the Death of a Dog" from HOW TO BE YOUR DOG'S BEST FRIEND. Little, Brown and Co, 1978.

Sife, Wallace, THE LOSS OF A PET. Howell Book House, 1993.

Smith, Penelope, "Matters of Life and Death" and "When a Great One Dies" from ANIMALS...OUR RETURN TO WHOLENESS, Pegasus Publications, 1993.

There are many more books available to help you in your personal experience. Reading helps take you out of your grief for a time, and that helps you heal. Consult your library and local (including church) bookstores.

Great Spiritual Power of the Universe,
turn your sun on in my life
so that I may reflect it back to you.

Self-Help Resources

The following list of resources can be used for more information about recovery options for issues surrounding death and bereavement, addictions, health concerns, or problems related to dysfunctional families. The addresses and telephone numbers listed are for the national headquarters; look in your local yellow pages under "Community Services" for resources closer to your area.

In addition to the following groups, other self-help organizations may be available in your area to assist your healing and recovery for a particular life crisis not listed here. Consult your telephone directory, call a counseling center or help line near you, or write or call:

American Self-Help Clearinghouse
St. Clares-Riverside
Medical Center
Denville, NJ 07834
(201) 625-7101

National Self-Help Clearinghouse
25 West 43rd St., Room 620
New York, NY 10036
(212) 642-2944

Aids

AIDS Hotline
(800) 342-2437

**Children with AIDS
Project of America**
4020 N. 20th St., Ste. 101
Phoenix, AZ 85016
(602) 265-4859
Hotline
(602) 843-8654

**The Names Project -
AIDS Quilt**
(800) 872-6263

National AIDS Network
(800) 342-2437

**National Association for
People with AIDS**
2025 "I" St. NW, Ste. 1101
Washington, DC 20006
(202) 429-2856

Project Inform
19655 Market St., Ste. 220
San Francisco, CA 94103
(415) 558-8669

PWA Coalition
50 W. 17th St.
New York, NY 10011

Spanish AIDS Hotline
(800) 344-7432

**TDD (Hearing Impaired)
AIDS Hotline**
(800) 243-7889

Alcohol Abuse

Al-Anon Family Headquarters
200 Park Ave. South
New York, NY 10003
(212) 302-7240

Alcoholics Anonymous (AA)
General Service Office
475 Riverside Dr.
New York, NY 10115
(212) 870-3400

**Children of Alcoholics
Foundation**
P.O. Box 4185
Grand Central Station
New York, NY 10163-4185
(212) 754-0656
(800) 359-COAF

Meridian Council, Inc.
Administrative Offices
4 Elmcrest Terrace
Norwalk, CT 06850

**National Association of
Children of Alcoholics
(NACOA)**
11426 Rockville Pike, Ste. 100
Rockville, MD 20852
(301) 468-0985

**National Clearinghouse for
Alcohol and Drug Information
(NCADI)**
P.O. Box 234
Rockville, MD 20852
(301) 468-2600

**National Council on
Alcoholism and Drug
Dependency (NCADD)**
12 West 21st St.
New York, NY 10010
(212) 206-6770

Anorexia/Bulimia

**American Anorexia/Bulimia
Association, Inc.**
418 East 76th St.
New York, NY 10021
(212) 891-8686

**Bulimic/Anorexic
Self-Help (BASH)**
P.O. Box 39903
St. Louis, MO 63138
(800) 888-4680

Eating Disorder Organization
1925 East Dublin Granville Rd.
Columbus, OH 43229-3517
(614) 436-1112

Cancer

National Cancer Institute
(800) 4-CANCER

Commonweal
P.O. Box 316
Bolinas, CA 94924
(415) 868-0971

**ECAP (Exceptional
Cancer Patients)**
Bernie S. Siegel, M.D.
300 Plaza Middlesex
Middletown, CT 06457
(800) 700-8869

CHILDREN'S ISSUES

Child Molestation

**Adults Molested As
Children United (AMACU)**
232 East Gish Rd.
San Jose, CA 95112
(800) 422-4453

**National Committee for
Prevention of Child Abuse**
322 South Michigan Ave.
Ste. 1600, Chicago, IL 60604
(312) 663-3520

Children's and Teens' Crisis Intervention

Boy's Town Crisis Hotline
(800) 448-3000

Covenant House Hotline
(800) 999-9999

Kid Save
(800) 543-7283

**National Runaway and
Suicide Hotline**
(800) 621-4000

Missing Children

Childsearch
Six Beacon St.
Boston, MA 02108
(617) 720-1760

Missing Children-Help Center
410 Ware Blvd., Ste. 400
Tampa, FL 33619
(800) USA-KIDS

**National Center for Missing
and Exploited Children**
1835 K St. NW
Washington, DC 20006
(800) 843-5678

Terminally Ill Children (fulfilling wishes)

Brass Ring Society
7020 S. Yale Ave., Ste. 103
Tulsa, OK 74136
(918) 496-2838

**The Candlelighters Childhood
Cancer Foundation**
1901 Pennsylvania Ave. NW
Ste. 1001
Washington, DC 20006
(202) 659-5136

A Wish with Wings
P.O. Box 110418
Arlington, TX 76007
(817) 261-8752

Co-Dependency

Co-Dependents Anonymous
P.O. Box 33577
Phoenix, AZ 85067-3577
(602) 277-7991

Death/Grieving/Suicide

**American Association of
Suicidology**
2459 South Ash St.
Denver, CO 80222
(303) 692-0985

Concern for Dying
250 W. 57th St.
New York, NY 10107
(212) 246-6962

**Forum for Death Education
and Counsel (FDEC)**
2211 Arthur Ave.
Lakewood, OH 44107
(216) 228-0334

Grief Recovery Helpline
(800) 445-4808

Grief Recovery Institute
8306 Wilshire Blvd., Ste. 21A
Beverly Hills, CA 90211
(213) 650-1234

**Mothers Against Drunk
Driving (MADD)**
669 Airport Freeway, Ste. 310
Hurst, TX 76053
(817) 268-6233

**National Hospice Organization
(NHO)**
1901 N. Ft. Myer Dr., Ste. 402
Arlington, VA 22209
(703) 243-5900

**National Sudden Infant Death
Syndrome**
Two Metro Plaza, Ste. 205
Landover, MD 20785
(800) 221-SIDS

Parents of Suicides
15 E. Brinkerhoff Ave.
Palisades Park, NJ 07650
(201) 585-7608

Seasons: Suicide Bereavement
4777 Naniola Dr.
Salt Lake City, UT 84117

Widowed Persons Service
1909 K St., NW
Washington, DC 20049
(202) 872-4700

Debts

Diabetes

Debtors Anonymous
General Service Office
P.O. Box 400
Grand Central Station
New York, NY 10163-0400
(212) 642-8220

American Diabetes Association
(800) 232-3472

Drug Abuse

Cocaine Anonymous
(800) 347-8998

National Cocaine-Abuse Hotline
(800) 262-2463
(800) COCAINE

National Institute of Drug Abuse (NIDA)
Parklawn Building
5600 Fishers Lane, Room 10A-39
Rockville, MD 20852
(301) 443-6245 (for information)
(800) 662-4357 (for help)

World Service Office (NA)
P.O. Box 9999
Van Nuys, CA 91409
(818) 780-3951

Eating Disorders

Food Addiction Hotline
Florida Institute of Technology
FIT Hotline
Drug Addiction & Depression
(800) 872-0088

Overeaters Anonymous
National Office
Rio Rancho, NM
(505) 891-2664

Gambling

Gamblers Anonymous
National Council on
Compulsive Gambling
444 West 59th St., Room 1521
New York, NY 10019
(212) 265-8600

Health Issues

**Alzheimer's Disease
Information**
(800) 621-0379

**American Chronic Pain
Association**
P.O. Box 850
Rocklin, CA 95677
(916) 632-0922

**American Foundation of
Traditional Chinese Medicine**
1280 Columbus Ave., Ste. 302
San Francisco, CA 94133
(415) 776-0502

**American Holistic Health
Association**
P.O. Box 17400
Anaheim, CA 92817
(714) 779-6152

**Center for Human Potential
and Mind-Body Medicine**
Deepak Chopra, M.D.
973 B Lomas Santa Fe Dr.
Solana Beach, CA 92075
(619) 794-2425

The Fetzer Institute
9292 West KL Ave.
Kalamazoo, MI 49009
(616) 375-2000

Hippocrates Health Institute
1443 Palmdale Court
West Palm Beach, FL 33411
(407) 471-8876

Hospicelink
(800) 331-1620

Institute for Noetic Sciences
P.O. Box 909, Dept. M
Sausalito, CA 94966-0909
(800) 383-1394

The Mind-Body Medical Institute
185 Pilgrim Rd.
Boston, MA 02215
(617) 732-7000

National Health Information Center
P.O. Box 1133
Washington, DC 20013-1133
(800) 336-4797

Optimum Health Care Institute
6970 Central Ave.
Lemon Grove, CA 91945
(619) 464-3346

Preventive Medicine Institute
Dean Ornish, M.D.
900 Bridgeway, Ste. 2
Sausalito, CA 94965
(415) 332-2525

World Research Foundation
15300 Ventura Blvd., Ste. 405
Sherman Oaks, CA 91403
(818) 907-5483

Impotence

Impotency Institute of America
2020 Pennsylvania Ave. N.W.,
Ste. 292
Washington, DC 20006
(800) 669-1603

Incest

Incest Survivors Resource Network International, Inc.
P.O. Box 7375
Las Cruces, NM 88006-7375
(505) 521-4260

Pet Bereavement

Bide-A-Wee Foundation
New York, NY
(212) 532-6395

The Animal Medical Center
New York, NY
(212) 838-8100

Holistic Animal Consulting Center
Staten Island, NY
(718) 720-5548

Rape

Austin Rape Crisis Center
1824 East Oltorf
Austin, TX 78741
(512) 440-7273

Sex Addictions

National Council on Sexual Addictions
P.O. Box 652
Azle, TX 76098-0652
(800) 321-2066

Smoking Abuse

Nicotine Anonymous
2118 Greenwich St.
San Francisco, CA 94123
(415) 750-0328

Spousal Abuse

National Coalition Against
Domestic Violence
P.O. Box 34103
Washington, DC 20043-4103
(202) 638-6388
(800) 333-7233 (crisis line)

Stress Reduction

The Biofeedback &
Psychophysiology Clinic
The Menninger Clinic
P.O. Box 829
Topeka, KS 66601-0829
(913) 273-7500

New York Open Center
(In-depth workshops to
invigorate the spirit)
83 Spring St.
New York, NY 10012
(212) 219-2527

Omega Institute
(A healing, spiritual
retreat community)
260 Lake Dr.
Rhinebeck, NY 12572-3212
(914) 266-4444 (info)
(800) 944-1001 (to enroll)

Rise Institute
P.O. Box 2733
Petaluma, CA 94973
(707) 765-2758

The Stress Reduction Clinic
Jon Kabat-Zinn, Ph.D.
University of Massachusetts
Medical Center
55 Lake Avenue North
Worcester, MA 01655
(508) 856-1616

In this sad world of ours, sorrow comes to all,
and it often comes with bitter agony. Perfect relief
is not possible, except with time. You cannot now
believe that you will ever feel better. But this is not
true. You are sure to be happy again. Knowing this,
truly believing it, will make you less miserable now.
I have had enough experience to make this statement.

— Abraham Lincoln

May you live all the days of your life.

— Jonathan Swift

ABOUT THE AUTHOR

Elizabeth A. Johnson holds a Master of Arts degree in Mass Communications from the American University in Washington, D.C. For a number of years, she was involved with both the entertainment industry and arts-in-education programs in New York, Miami, and Los Angeles. A long-time student of Eastern and Western movement and philosophy, she is a certified T'ai Chi instructor, as well as a jazz and tap dancer.

Sometime ago, Elizabeth had the precious opportunity to be with a family member when he died. That profound experience motivated the writing of *As Someone Dies*...and a subsequent series of ongoing lectures and workshops on the transformation and graduation process.

We hope you enjoyed this Hay House book.
If you would like to receive a free catalog featuring
additional Hay House books and products,
or if you would like information about the
Hay Foundation, please write to:

Hay House, Inc.
P.O. Box 6204
1154 E. Dominguez St.
Carson, CA 90749-6204

or call:

(800) 654-5126